Finding God
in Everyday Life

Richard A. Boever, C.SS.R.

LIGUORI
PUBLICATIONS

One Liguori Drive
Liguori, Missouri 63057
(314) 464-2500

Imprimi Potest:
Stephen T. Palmer, C.SS.R.
Provincial, St. Louis Province
Redemptorist Fathers

Imprimatur:
+ Edward J. O'Donnell
Vicar General, Archdiocese of St. Louis

ISBN 0-89243-285-3
Library of Congress Catalog Card Number: 87-83612

Excerpts taken from the NEW AMERICAN BIBLE with the
REVISED NEW TESTAMENT copyright © 1986 by the Con-
fraternity of Christian Doctrine, Washington, D.C. 20005,
are used with permission. All rights reserved.

Table of Contents

Foreword

Turn on the power switch of even the most primitive radio and begin rotating the tuning knob. Chances are you will hear a variety of music. The better the receiver and antenna, the more possibility you will have of finding the kind of music to delight your taste. But turn off the radio, and all the music, good and bad, will cease.

A radio without an energy source ceases to play music, but it doesn't end the broadcast. The radio waves continue to bounce through the atmosphere. Though undetected by us, they are there. This analogy applies to our attempts to find God in our world.

The most primitive "I believe" is like turning on the radio. God broadcasts, but until we open ourselves to receive his message it is very possible not to hear him. Taking the first step of giving God the chance to break through is like turning on the radio energy source. But it is only the beginning. We have to follow up with the fine tuning. In terms of this analogy, there are many stations available. We may tune in our parents' or teachers' station, for instance, and feel uncomfortable with it. That challenges us to search further, listening to a variety of styles but searching for the one that we can understand. This process is the struggle of bringing the "I believe" from an *acceptance of creed* to *the experience of God*. That requires not only hearing God but also the even finer tuning of eliminating the static and utilizing the full power of the station.

When we move from ''I believe the facts of religion'' to ''I may not be able to prove anything to you but I KNOW A LOVING GOD,'' life takes on new meaning.

The first part of this booklet examines how God speaks to each one of us. The second part considers our response to God. These two elements, listening to God and responding to the Lord, are what we call spirituality. Thus we have here a short ''handbook of spirituality'' which has been entitled **Finding God in Everyday Life** because living a Christian spirituality means answering the call to live God's life at all times.

There is something about our Christian faith that demands full human growth in order to experience full spiritual life. Though we often divide these issues to zero in on a concept, the two go together. Before God can give us all the blessings he wishes to bestow, we must be fully alive to human life; and before we can truly know full human life, we must be spiritual people. Until we experience the fact that we are lovable — for instance, through the love of those around us — we will never know the love of God, though we may believe it as an article of faith. By the same token, if we do not experience the love of God after we experience the love of others, we won't know the fullness of how lovable we truly are. Thus, growth in the spiritual life is human growth; and human growth, even without sprinkling it with holy water, is true spiritual growth.

The goal of this booklet, then, is to present a simple handbook of spirituality by considering how to live a full life.

PART ONE

GOD SPEAKS
TO US

CHAPTER 1

Our Belief in God

Not all people believe in the same way. Some, for example, decide not to trust that God is present in the very ordinary; they cannot make the leap to believe it is possible to have contact with God. Others believe that God *is* present in the very ordinary; and, though they cannot actually prove their belief, it is a major tenet of their creed. Consequently, some freely choose to believe God is in events; others freely choose not to believe.

To believe or not to believe, that's the real issue. There's nothing new in the great standoff of faith. For instance, the great theologian Saint Thomas Aquinas knew that he could not prove the existence of God even though he listed five convincing arguments to substantiate his position. For those who believe, faith is not unreasonable; for those who do not believe, however, the "proofs" carry little weight.

It is easy to understand the mental attitudes of believers and agnostics. At least their positions make sense. But those who combine the two opposite positions — called *pious* agnostics — are hard to understand.

An agnostic is one who believes that God exists but that we can't really understand anything about him and there is certainly no contact with him. Some Christians are pious agnostics because they believe that although God exists he cannot be contacted; but just to play it on the safe side, they continue to say some prayers and practice some religion. They are not really interested in finding God and would just as soon he stayed in heaven, but they aren't going to take a chance. And chances are, as long as they maintain this position, they never will find God in their lives, even while they go through all the motions.

Good Christians are not pious agnostics. We want to know God in our lives. That's why this book is being written. We want to consider how God can be with us in our ordinary Christian lives.

The first thing each of us must do if we hope to hear God is to develop ears of faith. The bigger our ears, the more we can hear. Without this vital equipment, we will hear little.

To have ears of faith is to have that ability to know the presence of God in the ''coincidences'' of life. Though we may never be able to prove our conviction that what we believe to be God's message to us is really that, the coincidences of our lives put flesh and blood on the skeleton of our theology. If we limit our relationship with God to theology alone, the heart will never be captivated by the love of God. Our faith which seeks understanding needs more than just logic; it needs experiences of God.

There is a story told of a young girl whose hand was asked for in marriage by the ''perfect gentleman.'' She knew he was handsome, intelligent, well-bred, popular, and even very much in love with her. The girl's parents were thrilled by the proposal; she was envied by all her friends; and she presumed he would make as nearly a perfect husband as could be possible. There was only one problem: She didn't love him. She could list all his good qualities, but she didn't feel anything for him and, as a result, she could not accept his offer of marriage. Without knowing the love of God for us, we might be convinced of the goodness of God, but we will never be converted.

Our spiritual journey is primarily our ever-deepening experience of God in daily life. It's progressive. God is infinite and there's so much to find out about his infinite love that growth in the God-life will never end. That's probably what we'll be doing all of our eternity — finding out just how much God loves us.

Saint John the Evangelist gives us an indication of how our own progress will take place in the passage of the call of the disciples. There he telescopes his theology of vocation: it unfolds one layer after another:

> The next day John [the Baptizer] was there again with two of his disciples, and as he watched Jesus walk by, he said, "Behold, the Lamb of God." The two disciples heard what he said and followed Jesus. Jesus turned and saw them following him and said to them, "What are you looking for?" They said to him, "Rabbi" (which translated means Teacher), "where are you staying?" He said to them, "Come, and you will see." So they went and saw where he was staying, and they stayed with him that day . . . (John 1:35-39).

As the Baptizer's disciples were attracted by Jesus, so, too, something about the Lord intrigues us. This is a call from God. We are moved to search out this movement of our heart. And the Lord responds to our interest by inviting us to look further. He doesn't list his attributes; he lets us discover them ourselves by calling us to "Come and see."

The disciples themselves (in John 1:38,41,45,49,51) discovered the Lord step by step. First they knew him as a Teacher; then, progressively, as Messiah; the one Moses spoke about; the Son of God; and finally, the most important of all, the Son of Man who will be the point of communication between heaven and earth. "You shall see the sky opened and the angels of God ascending and descending on the Son of Man."

11

Earth and heaven are joined in Jesus. The experience of the disciples and all followers of Jesus, however, is that this is a conclusion reached only after many lived experiences. "Step by step," the Black spiritual rings out, "we are marching to Zion, step by step all the way."

In our coming to know the Lord, Saint John also hints at a spectacular and wonderful thing that happens to the believer. We come to know not only the Lord but also ourselves! Andrew and Philip became the evangelizers who bring Simon and Nathaniel respectively to Jesus (verses 41 and 45), Simon's very name was changed to Cephas as an illustration of how meeting Jesus touched him (verse 42), Nathaniel is identified as the true Israelite (verse 47), and the disciples are radically changed from being fishermen to fishers of men.

The same dynamics are operative today in the journey to God. The fact is that life can change; but the wearying circumstances of life can be integrated because we know the Lord is our great motivation to take the journey.

Personal considerations

1. Are you willing to let the Lord "talk to you" through the experiences of your day, or do you hold that God is in heaven while you have to live on earth and that you can't meet him until after death?

2. Spend ten minutes alone trying to experience your gift of faith. This is an exercise of the heart; whenever you begin to think of the content of faith (the things you believe) dismiss those thoughts. Simply know with your inner sense that you believe.

CHAPTER 2
God's World

"Ever since the creation of the world, his invisible attributes of eternal power and divinity have been able to be understood and perceived in what he has made" (Romans 1:20). Saint Paul glories in the many possibilities available to find God in *this* world. He doesn't call for a withdrawal from life to make room for the eternal.

Most of us, at one time or another, have been struck by the grandeur of a sunset or the beauty of a landscape. It is wonderful to behold the order, the power, the intricacy of our world. In that moment of inspiration we might have even found our thoughts drifting toward the Creator. We might have felt, somewhere in the depth of our being, a prayer of thanks, as though the scene had been placed there simply as our gift for that moment. At those times we can experience, if only for a fleeting second, a closeness to God. We experience a sense of awe.

Becoming aware of God in creation is not always so simple. Sometimes the uplifting experience is rather short-lived. In the midst of the experience of God in nature, a skepticism can creep in, trying to convince us that we have made a jump in logic. We might hear ourselves saying that the landscape would have been beautiful regardless of whether or not we were there to witness it.

We need not deny that. The real challenge is not in the contact with the external beauty in itself but in making the leap to believe that God can and did touch us through that beauty. And we must admit that takes faith.

Creation is not given to us to be grasped. It exists, in a very real sense, independent of us. In fact, holding too tightly to the beauty short-circuits the wonder and is the cause of many of our modern materialistic problems. That kind of possessiveness of creation limits rather than expands our awareness. It makes us selfish and controlling of others who need to share in the richness of the earth for their survival. It mistakes the gift for the Giver. The physical creation and the beauty are not God — they are means of experiencing him.

Because creation is the work of God and is a reflection of him, it is possible to experience him in it as a husband is able to see the reflection of his wife in the beauty of their children. The child is not the wife, but the tilt of the head of the child or the phrase used to express a thought brings a sudden feeling of awareness that the child is a reflection of the parents' love.

The reflections of God's world cannot be held for long. They are intuitions that the Creator is speaking to those who are able to hear. The physical matter is not the essence of the gift; it is only the vehicle of the communication with God, who speaks his love through it. Blindness to this fact can interfere with our vision of God.

Seeing the manifestation of the love of God in the wonder of creation is different. It keeps things in proper perspective. The world was created and judged "good" by God. It reflects the Creator and is entrusted to us to be used, not possessed, as a means to become our best possible selves. We are the stewards, not the manipulators of creation.

Pierre Teilhard de Chardin, a priest-scientist, captured the Christian attitude toward creation in his book *The Divine Milieu*.

He reminds us that on some given day we may suddenly become conscious that we are alive to a particular perception of the divine spread everywhere about us. He writes of himself: "There is a sense in which he [Christ] is at the tip of my pen — of my heart and of my thought." Together with Christ, aware persons take the clay of matter and, working with the Christ who redeemed the entire world, build the kingdom of God by the work of their hands.

This story about a certain saint makes the same point. When he walked through the woods with the aid of his cane, he saw God's presence everywhere. He tapped the wild flowers lightly and admonished them: "Hush, hush," he would say, "you speak too loudly to me of the love of God, and I must be about my business." Many others passed through the woods in haste, unaware of the vehicle it provided to hear the voice of God.

The experience of God in creation can be varied. It might be his power or his order or his beauty that we touch. It also might be fleeting, lasting only a moment; but the union is real, not because the physical matter is God but because God is able to use the things of this world to communicate himself to us.

Personal considerations

1. Consider how creation exists without you and how it cannot actually be possessed.

2. Using ordinary crayons and plain paper, express an experience of awe which you have felt through the beauty of creation by drawing a picture of the experience.

CHAPTER 3
God in Others

When Jesus talked about the kingdom of God, he was not at all slow to teach his disciples of the close connection between the realm of the eternal and the reality of our day-to-day grind. The most direct association of "the two worlds" was made obvious by the Lord in the lesson on the Last Judgment, recorded in Matthew — a familiar passage to every Christian. Those who had one foot in eternal life were the ones who cared enough to demonstrate their concern to a brother or sister in need. When the Great Judge points out this fact, the just say: " 'Lord, when did we see you hungry and feed you, or thirsty and give you drink? When did we see you a stranger and welcome you, or naked and clothe you? When did we see you ill or in prison, and visit you?' And the king will say to them in reply, 'Amen, I say to you, whatever you did for one of these least brothers of mine, you did for me' " (Matthew 25:37-40).

From this teaching we can see a number of important elements concerning our communion with God. The first, and most obvious, is this: The Lord is not saying that only in heroic action is there contact with God. An action as simple as a parent getting a child a glass of water receives the merit of giving drink to the thirsty. It is also clear that the union with God through other people is not always conscious. Many of the interactions with other people will not bear direct messages from God. The just in Matthew's account were unaware of taking care of the needs of the Lord when they cared for others, even though it was the reason for their reward. (In reality, it may not be the doer of the good deed who hears the message of the love of God but the receiver. The child who receives the drink of water, for instance, has an opportunity to become aware of the loving concern of the Father through the kindness more so than the parent, who may only feel irritation at the inconvenience of the request.) But there is no doubt that our good deeds have one foot in heaven: "As often as you do it . . . "

In our human interactions, we *can* hear the voice of God. Here is an example from the life of a certain priest: Once I gave a homily that was not well received, largely due to my own self-righteousness. It was rather hard-hitting, and my parishioners let me know it was very unpopular. I took their criticism to heart. That evening I was in our chapel praying and discussing the issue with God. (Actually, I was feeling sorry for myself and complaining that the Lord was not very supportive.) A child I knew came into the chapel while her parents were talking with one of the other priests. She sat on my lap, gave me a hug, and said, "Thank you." I didn't understand the words, and so I said, "Thank you for what, Jennifer?" She responded, "Thank you for you." Then she got up and left.

That was a very ordinary occurrence. Kids do that all the time. Nothing very startling had taken place. But for some reason or another, the moment was significant to this priest at the time and no doubt still is. The words of the child were an answer to his prayer. It was the message he needed to hear God say at that moment; and, for him, Jennifer spoke God's words.

Were these words from God? For him, at that time, they were. And why couldn't they have been that? Did not the Lord assure us that where two or more are gathered in his name, he would be present? We do not have to conjure up the Lord's presence in our relationships. He is there. What we have to do is become aware and believe!

This example of the exchange with Jennifer is merely a whisper of the voice of God when compared to some of the encounters that take place between human beings. This, in fact, is the center of the theology of Christian marriage: "Be Christ to one another!"

None of us grows in a vacuum. Our very self-concept is formed, in large part, by what others have told us. If they love us, we can believe we are lovable; if not, we doubt our self-worth. So much of counseling is processing and, if need be, reordering the lessons we have learned. If such awareness is necessary for psychological health, why should we think things are different in coming to know our true spiritual selves?

It is not different. Our very concept of God, for example, is formed at least partially by what we have learned from our parents. Jesus called God Abba, that is, Daddy. Saint John stated the fact simply: "If anyone says, 'I love God,' but hates his brother, he is a liar; for whoever does not love a brother whom he has seen cannot love God whom he has not seen" (1 John 4:20). The two — God and the human family — are very closely connected, and God speaks to us through the words and actions of our brothers and sisters and to those around us through our words.

Personal considerations

1. Have you ever thanked God for answering your prayers through the words or actions of another?

2. Look through your collection of photographs of family and friends and think how they have influenced the way you act in your present life and how you think of God today. These experiences will probably include both positive and negative influences on you.

CHAPTER 4

God and
Our Inner Selves

There is within our minds a constant conversation with ourselves. A lot of it is useless chatter and it takes great discipline and practice to silence those monologues to allow for deeper reflection and prayer. On the other hand, motivated by our feelings and aided by our imagination, our thoughts help us to sort out the events of daily life. These thoughts affect our view of life and they are important. A great deal of our emotional health depends on how we think, what we feel, and how we use our imagination.

Our Thoughts

When our thought process becomes distorted, we can cause ourselves unnecessary pain. Correcting cognitive distortions is essential to feeling good. The Bible instructs us to look to the voices of our minds and hearts in the quest for God and the peace that this relationship brings.

"I will put my laws in their minds
   and I will write them upon their hearts.

I will be their God,
and they shall be my people'' (Hebrews 8:10).
God can be found in our own thoughts because his laws are already in our minds and within our hearts.

In a famous play about Joan of Arc, the saint is on trial as a witch after having brought victory to the armies she led according to the voices she heard in her own mind. The prosecutors, who were defeated by Joan's army, condemn her as being possessed by the devil; Joan claims that the voices were from God, but there is no way she can prove it, especially to a court made up of the enemy.

At one point, Joan is visited by a dear friend who would like to see her freed from the certain death sentence a conviction of demon-possession would bring. He argues with her that the voices are only her own thoughts. She agrees to that fact; he hopes that she might be released. But it was not to be. Joan asserts that the voices were her own thoughts but that God spoke through them.

As it was for Saint Joan, so the task is for each one of us to decipher what God is saying to us in our own inner world of thoughts, feelings, and imagination. The word most often used to describe this process is discernment, which is the reading of the movements of our hearts and a decision to choose a course of action leading toward God. Discernment is very holy and also very human. It presumes the grace of God, but it also requires common sense, a good deal of self-knowledge and spiritual sensitivity.

Saint Ignatius of Loyola, the most famous teacher of the rules of discernment, makes it very clear that this can be a confusing area. Even the most insightful and holy person often requires the aid of a spiritual adviser who can help test the conclusions in the more cloudy issues. But most of our discernments are done privately in the inner workings of our own spirits.

The issue that clouds our discernments is the fact that we are good at rationalizing our wrong decisions, justifying even evil actions, fooling ourselves that bad is good. We have to be honest with ourselves. God gave us a destiny and a calling to greatness. Sin is the failure to become all that we were created to be, but in Christ we can rise above our smallness and become human persons fully alive.

Really to hear God we have to filter and refine our thoughts to remove the dross. This requires looking at what is being heard and seeing the choices the voices of our minds place before us. It calls for the work of weighing the pros and cons of alternate courses of actions, trying to remain neutral to the ramifications of a particular decision, but weighing the feelings that move us. And it requires prayer for enlightenment and confirmation of our decision by the people around us, especially those who have special claim to our allegiance. Discernment is filtering the many words our minds and hearts speak and deciding which are from God.

The question is not whether God actually speaks to us in our inner world but which of the many messages are his. The voice of God manifested in our own thoughts, though it does require diligent effort of our human faculties, is powerful. It carries with it assurance of a special communication to us as individuals. It is the message of God for us, in the particular circumstances of our lives, for this specific time. It is a blessing.

Our Feelings

Feelings, too, are part of our inner world and speak the voice of God. They run the gamut from delight to despair. They may show up uninvited and be completely unexpected, or they may be the normal pattern in particular circumstances. We may, for instance, be surprised that a promotion at work causes us more sadness at leaving our friends than happiness in the new prestige. Then again, we may be well aware that we see red every time an associate makes a racist comment.

Feelings may even surface that are inappropriate for the situation. They may not be "now" feelings because they emerge from the memory banks we all have. For instance, a feeling of abandonment may cause a person to panic. Such a response is appropriate for a child who could not survive if he or she were abandoned; an adult, however, has a number of options open to handle the situation. But the feeling is real nonetheless.

Feelings, they say, are neither good nor bad. They're just there. But that doesn't mean they aren't important nor does it mean that they should just be left "there." They have to be faced. Pop-psychology states that if we can name a feeling, we can tame it. Feelings have a great deal to do with our state of well-being. And, as we might expect, feelings figure into our contact with God and have to be a part of our spiritual life.

Sometimes our feelings give pleasure, sometimes they give pain. We welcome the ones that feel good, like joy and peace; but negative feelings, like despair and envy, make us uncomfortable. Both the positive and negative feelings have a place in our spiritual journey; they can put us in contact with God, but we have to understand them.

Being consoled usually means that we are going in the right direction — toward God; being in desolation doesn't necessarily mean that we have made a wrong turn. If our orientation is that of a maturing Christian — our basic direction in life is toward God — the consolations we receive are from God who wants us to keep going. But if our direction is away from God, the resulting desolation challenges us to return to him. Therefore, before we can make any judgment about our consolations or desolations, we have to know in what direction our lives are headed. Then we can hear what God is saying to us through our feelings.

The further point should also be remembered: Sometimes even those whose lives are God-oriented suffer desolation in the midst of consolation. If this happens to us, what should we do? Consolation is easy to accept: Enjoy it, giving the credit to God! Desolation is not so easy to handle because it can hurt. If we are truly living life as we know God would want it lived, we endure desolation as coming from the mysterious hand of God. We intensify rather than decrease our spiritual efforts; we suffer in patience.

Desolation is part of the mystery of God in our lives. It is a point of contact with God, as is consolation. Our feelings carry a message from God. Saint Paul, for instance, knew he was following the call of God in his life, yet the desolation he experienced made it all the more real for him:

> We hold this treasure in earthen vessels, that the surpassing power may be of God and not from us. We are afflicted in every way, but not constrained; perplexed, but not driven to despair; persecuted, but not abandoned; struck down, but not destroyed; always carrying about in the body the dying of Jesus, so that the life of Jesus may also be manifested in our body. For we who live are constantly being given up to death for the sake of Jesus, so that the life of Jesus may be manifested in our mortal flesh (2 Corinthians 4:7-11).

Our Imagination

Children have fantastic imaginations. At night, a light shining through a window, casting monstrous, grotesque figures on a darkened mirror can spark fear in their imaginations. In the full light of day, the images disappear, but in the darkness of night they seem exceedingly real.

Not all imagination involves monsters and danger, of course. It can also include the fantasy of a sand castle, the power of a cardboard box train, the companionship of make-believe friends. Persons who imagine don't necessarily believe that the images are real, but they have the right to pretend they are. Their imaginings represent deeper truths — that there is something more than physical reality.

Here is the way a creative convert wrote about imagination in his experience of Church: "I decided that I needed to change my image of pilgrim Church, with its emphasis on *grim* to that of *gypsy* church. Like all good gypsies, I could delight in sitting around the campfire and spinning stories with my imagination. My eyes could twinkle, reflecting my soul. And maybe one morning I would wake, realizing that the road I was traveling had led me to Emmaus."

Images are important to all we think and do. They are like the house foundation that we ignore until there is a leak in the basement. They are the unseen support that determines the external structures we build with our words and thoughts. They are important ways God speaks to us.

Pretending can be a way of bringing the intuitive dimension of faith into consciousness. Our society emphasizes logic and intellectual constructs, but we will never be able to experience the depth of religion with thought alone. Imagination is a direct route to the heart of religion. Good and evil, love and hate, victory and defeat, can be more immediately known in the imaginary sword fight between two children with scraps of wood as weapons than through a treatise on the subject. The imagination offers communion with the topic at hand. It is experienced rather than defined.

Imagination is the inner realm of life that determines so much else. This is the level of myth, the truths too deep to express in narrative. It is more than "what is." It is the intuitive understanding of the human condition and God's involvement with this daily reality.

Listening to God in our imagination means being sensitive to the symbols of our lives, to allow ourselves to dream and to fantasize, and to pray prayers that are "useless" except that they place us in the presence of God and at the center of ourselves, to draw pictures expressing experience. It may have no purpose. It leads to no resolutions. It calls for no change. But it probes the very depth of awareness. It is the experience of the holy and an essential part in meeting God.

Personal considerations

1. Set aside five minutes to listen to your inner world and to realize how much activity goes on inside you — your thoughts, your feelings, your imagination. After the five minutes have passed, write down as many of the thoughts, feelings, and imaginations you can remember. Do you spend enough time listening to the voices within you?

2. Pretend that you are going to befriend some wild animal to accompany you in the present events of your life. What animal would you choose? What kind of behavior do you expect? How would it be a help to you? Why did you choose the animal you did?

3. Have you ever stopped to think that your thoughts, feelings, and imaginings are the way God has gifted you to work out your questions of life, and that God speaks to you by using them to help you come to decisions in life?

CHAPTER 5
God and
Our Human Nature

There is a strong suspicion for many modern Christians that God doesn't really have much to say to us through our human nature or our physical bodies. The roots of this doubt go way back into ancient philosophies that consider the body to be the prison of the soul. The basic presumption of this thought is that the body hinders true spiritual progress. As a matter of fact, the very word "spiritual" usually refers to things that have to do with the nonmaterial; and the body is certainly material.

To illustrate the point: During one Advent season, a Catholic publishing firm produced a children's educational bulletin about the relationship between Joseph and Mary before she was with child and noted the sudden change the pregnancy brought to the relationship. Almost immediately the publisher received a letter of complaint: "Our principal and teachers found it very offensive and entirely out of line with the Church's teaching. The Church has always taught that Mary was a virgin and remained a virgin, so how could she and Joseph 'plan to raise a family' as your bulletin stated? We did not use the bulletin with the children, but I showed it to one parent who remarked 'Sounds like lust' when she read the line that said Joseph 'had gone to sleep that night to dream of his sweet Mary.' If Joseph and Mary were the kind of people that you described, I do not think that the Church would hold them up as models for us.''

The line was not, of course, contrary to the teachings of the Church. Joseph and Mary did indeed plan to marry and raise a family. It would have been contrary to their Jewish culture and religion (and to Catholic sacramental theology as well) to have been betrothed and not plan to have sexual relations with the intention of having children after marriage. After the angel's announcement, Joseph and Mary changed their plans in order to accept God's plan. Their willingness to follow his will — even though they did not completely understand and probably would not have chosen this way on their own — is the real reason to look to them as models after whom we can pattern our own behavior. Joseph and Mary's original thoughts were not lustful; they were filled with a very healthy and holy human love which included expressing that love physically.

But the suspicion of things physical is not surprising. Our past is riddled with more than objecting letters. Whole rituals of brutal flagellations of the body — some condemned by the Church — make up our past Western history.

We are slow to listen to God through our bodies. Deep down, we still doubt that God could use them for holy messages. As modern as we are, our expressions betray our split spirituality. For instance, doesn't even the phrase ''Listen to your body'' (which seems like an enlightened statement) really imply that the ''I'' is only residing in the body and that the body should be attended to when it rattles, like when the engine knocks in our automobiles? Certain recent studies of out-of-the-body experiences have alerted us to many surrounding realities of our universe; but we may be more in need of exploring our in-the-body experiences before anything else.

27

Though we can be aware that we are more than our bodies, it is difficult to think of ourselves without them. And why should we? It is an article of our faith that we believe our body will always be a part of us: "I believe in the resurrection of the body." And are not our bodies, earthen vessels though they be, the dwelling place of God? "Do you not know that your body is a temple of the holy Spirit within you, whom you have from God?" (1 Corinthians 6:19) If there was any doubt about the goodness of the body, it is dispelled in the wonder of the Incarnation. The Son of God took on our very nature which included a human body.

When God speaks to us in our bodies, we listen! When we disrespect our bodies, for instance, through any excess, our bodies will react and God's message to respect our bodies will be known in the ills we suffer. To abuse our bodies, as for instance to become such workaholics that we do not have time to follow a proper diet, is not of God. The body is the temple of the Holy Spirit.

As in all the points mentioned, health or illness does not have to put us in contact with God. Proper care of our bodies carries its own reward whether we believe in God or not. On the other hand, God can be present to us in our ordinary, prudent, physical life. But these messages are only the superficial contact. It goes much deeper.

In a very real sense, it is only in our body that we know life. It is by the work of our hands that we make something of our world. It is through our bodies that we are in union with other people. It is in our bodies that we think and feel and imagine. It is even in our bodies that we pray. God, as it were, needs our bodies to talk with us and we need them to be fully human.

Through our bodies we accomplish our tasks in life. A very close union with God is possible through this human activity, but to have contact with God in our tasks, we need the awareness that what we are doing is not only practical and necessary for survival but good in and of itself. The work itself is holy. The phrase "holy worldliness" applies here. Hungering and thirsting for God in this physical-spiritual sense is the call to become involved with our work and to believe it is part of the plan of God. Growing in this awareness is the call to imitate the Creator through all the seven days of creation, not just up to the completion of our tasks, but through the Sabbath.

We speak of the seven days of creation. The Book of Genesis shows that the "work of creation" was completed on the sixth day (or period of time). "On the seventh day God was finished with the work he had been doing" (Genesis 2:1). If our lives are merely work, without the seventh day we will never complete the week. It is important when we finish one task not to move on to the next project without reflection on the completed work. We might otherwise miss the meaning of the work: "God blessed the seventh day and made it holy, because on it he rested from all the work he had done in creation" (Genesis 2:3).

There is a danger that we will imitate the Creator's work only up to the sixth day. We will see our work and judge it good, but we won't experience the ultimate purpose of it — that it is holy. Contact with God demands that we not only perform our task but also sanctify it and so consecrate the task itself. It is what we are supposed to do now in accord with God's plan.

Personal considerations

1. Do you believe that your body is the temple of the Holy Spirit and do you, therefore, treat it with respect?

2. Do something good for your body today. Start an exercise program; quit smoking or drinking; get enough rest; take a warm bath.

CHAPTER 6
God's Providence

Thus far in our consideration of the development of our spiritual selves we have listened to God speaking to us through the world, the messages from people around us, and voices of thought, feeling, and imagination in our physical bodies. If all these beautiful experiences offer the possibility of hearing the voice of a loving God, does the presence of evil call for the existence of a devil? Is he responsible for the disasters of nature? For the people who are out to hurt? For those persons who are sick in body, in mind, or in spirit? For those desolate times when we experience the absence of God?

So often we say that God is good because we win the lottery or have a beautiful day or experience good health. But if we attribute the good things of life to a Supreme Being, wouldn't it be fair to blame God or some evil force for the bad things that happen to us? In fact, this is what people often do. When, for instance, a doctor diagnoses some horrible disease, the patient almost instinctively figures that God is punishing him or her for some sin of the past.

In this chapter we want to say something about the "bad" things in life that interfere with a comfortable existence.

Most of the time we lump together under the heading of "evil" the parts of our life that cause us to suffer. That is normal, but there are distinctions to be made that change the nature of the experience. For instance, the destruction of a tornado is different from the injury inflicted on a victim of crime. One involves the ordinary laws of nature, the other involves the contempt of human rights. Both cause pain, and we have a hard time with that. We look for some kind of explanation; we want to know where to place the blame.

Sometimes the cause of our suffering is not so difficult to discover. It is a direct consequence of our action. If, for instance, we are careless when using power tools, we run the risk of injury. But cause and effect are not always so obvious.

The classic reflection on evil is the impatient Job — found in Chapters 3–41 of the Old Testament book named after him. (The patient Job is found only in the chapters at the beginning and end of the book.) What makes the work so distinctive is that even though Job experienced every kind of evil — from the forces of nature, from the evil inflicted by other people, from confusion within himself, and even from an absent God — the author of this inspired work was unable to offer an acceptable explanation for Job's troubles. All the author could do was to reject the traditional answers of why Job had to suffer: "That's the way life is" (7:1-6 and 14:1-3); "suffering is a punishment for sin" (4:7-9 and 8:11-13); "suffering is for building character" (5:17-19 and 33:29-30); "suffering is meaningless" (21:23-26); and "suffering is mysterious" (42:2-3). In the end, when God finally speaks about evil, he doesn't give Job a solution. He only promises to "stand with" those who suffer (see Job, chapters 38-41).

It seems that most of us aren't too happy with God's response to Job. It isn't very satisfying. But it is honest, and it does jibe with our experiences of suffering.

The Bible is filled with laments. Look, for instance, at Psalm 13. The afflicted one cries out to God in uncouched graphics; the psalmist makes the complaint known. "How long, O Lord, will you utterly forget me?" Then comes the request: Do something before it is too late! "Lest my enemy say, 'I have overcome him.' " Finally, the last line ends in praise. Though we never know how long it took, the prayer was heard! "Let my heart rejoice in your salvation; let me sing of the Lord, 'He has been good to me.' "

We can't explain our suffering; but it need not conquer us and we need not be deluded by "disinformation." God does not manipulate the world or the events of our lives to get through to us. The fact of the matter is that God can be heard in every circumstance of our lives. The particular events are not important; hearing the message in them is. The difficult moments in life are just as important and just as filled with messages from God as are the more enjoyable experiences. In fact, to miss the voice of God in difficult times is to miss at least half of his messages. God speaks loudly in pain and it is important to spiritual maturity to listen to the Lord in those moments.

Paul's Letter to the Romans is an example. To him, the rejection of Christ by his own people was very painful, in fact an evil; but in it he was able to see that salvation was extended to the Gentiles. Paul was able to hear the voice of God even in this. "For if their rejection is the reconciliation of the world, what will their acceptance be? . . . If some of the branches were broken off, and you, a wild olive shoot, were grafted in their place and have come to share in the rich root of the olive tree, do not boast against the branches. . . . And they also, if they do not remain in unbelief, will be grafted in, for God is able to graft them in again" (Romans 11:15,17,23).

Personal considerations

1. Do you allow yourself to experience the depth of your pain, or do you seek to escape it at all cost?

2. Go to the library and check out a book which has pictured the great masterpieces of art. How many of them depict scenes of pain? What is their message?

3. Permit the pain in your life to be a part of you. God will speak through it.

CHAPTER 7

Our Contact
With God

Our ordinary human experiences and the functioning of the faculties with which we have been gifted by God are essential if we are to live spiritual lives. In a very real sense, to be fully human is to be holy. God speaks in many ways and it is our challenge to arrange our experiences of the sacred into an altar upon which we offer the sacrifice of our response. Literally, they become moments of "consecration," being "with the sacred." They indicate the way we keep in contact with God.

The Scriptures record how our ancestors in religion expressed their faith by building altars in order to commemorate and relive their faith experiences. Noah, for instance, built an altar to celebrate deliverance from the flood (Genesis 8:20). Abram built an altar "to the LORD . . . who had appeared to him" (Genesis 12:7). Jacob, Moses, David, and Elijah all built altars to worship the God with whom they had made contact (Genesis 35:1, Numbers 7:84, Judges 6:25, 2 Samuel 24:18, 1 Kings 18:30). Peter eloquently expressed what seems to be a natural response to such an experience when he cried out at the time of the Transfiguration of Jesus,

"It is good that we are here! Let us make three tents: one for you, one for Moses, and one for Elijah" (Mark 9:5).

There are meeting places with the sacred in our lives and we can "set aside" time to enter these arenas. External places where we can feel the sacred and respond with our prayer and sacrifice are important. For this reason, humankind has always erected temples, churches, and special places of worship. It even seems to be the experience of many that certain localities of themselves have an aura of holiness and when these places are consecrated and worship takes place there regularly, the presence is more profoundly felt.

The church buildings, however, are not the only places where we pray. At least equally important to us are the internal, personal altars where we meet God. The events and happenings of our lives offer the building material for these altars. A deep spirituality, like happiness, is a choice to spend the time and effort necessary to build them well. We live in a divine milieu, and a by-product of all we do is contact with the eminent God. Our spiritual journey is largely the art of becoming more sensitive to these experiences.

We should recall from time to time our experiences of God through creation, through encounters with others, through our own thoughts, feelings, imaginations, and even our physical bodies. The events themselves may have been pleasurable or difficult, but they should be considered as moments of consecration — times when we experienced being with the sacred.

These experiences make up the internal altar upon which we offer our worship to God. They are not stones of granite, but they are just as solid. Gathered together, they form the altars of our lives.

The preceding chapters of this booklet have examined how God speaks to each one of us. The following chapters will consider our response to God.

Personal considerations

This exercise is meant to summarize the first part of this booklet. Recall your personal experiences of God in creation, through others, in your thoughts, feelings, imaginations, and even in your body. These events might have been positive or negative experiences. Imagine that each experience is a stone. Draw these stones — labeled if you so desire with the experience they represent — side-by-side and row-upon-row to form an altar upon which your response, considered in the second part of this booklet, can be your sacrifice to God.

PART TWO

WE RESPOND TO GOD

CHAPTER 8
Adjusting to Current Culture

The foregoing cha pters of this booklet have not been extremely revolutionary or startling. Spirituality is simple. But when we look at spirituality more critically, we see that there is a definite challenge. What is our response to the God who is able to break through to us?

Each generation has to come to terms with its responses to God. Not only in past epics of history has this been true, but the evolution of modern thought and the cultural surroundings of today dictate that each era and each tribe will bring its peculiar insights to bear on its relationship with God. It is partially this interchange of the holy and the worldly that makes God personal. We are citizens of this nation at a particular time with an awareness formed by these group experiences passing through our own mental filters.

The Third World is shaping the theology of the universal Church in the modern world because it brings a unique experience of oppression and the liberation of the Savior to the Christian consciousness. The Church serves a vital function, and the theology is tightly bound with the society in which it functions. When these insights are shared by the universal Church, all members benefit from this expansion of awareness.

North America also has its unique experiences that give religious expression its own characteristics. The land evolved from a complex gathering of denominations and nationalities specifically determined to exercise religious freedom in an earthly society. The course of history continued to condition the experience, but the underlying foundation remains — that the Kingdom of God and earthly society are not mutually exclusive. Secular institutions, government, commerce, and technology are necessary practical realities, but they remain servants of the people, established not in their own right but as means toward fuller life. The very concept of separation of Church and state was primarily legislated as protection for *both* so that both could flourish to their full potential.

The natural question, fundamental to the North American consciousness, is this: "Why did God create the world?" The answer is optimistic. The Utopian and Transcendentalist movements indicate a preference for the belief that, because of the intent of the Creator and the redemption of the Savior and the indwelling of the Spirit, the world has the possibility of perfectibility.

To be authentic, our spirituality must take this preference into account. The advances of ecology or science or technology are not threats to spirituality; rather, they harmonize with the call to have dominion over the earth and to establish the kingdom of God. Since they contribute to the betterment of human life, they also contribute to holiness and the original mandate of the Creator to have dominion over the earth.

In the beginning, God created the human person to be good (see Genesis 1:27,31) though not perfect. This was a gift to be given only in the fullness of time. But there was a fall. Christ had to come: "For if immortality had remained invisible and unknown, then it would have not brought us salvation'' (Saint Ireneaus). Jesus assumed the original nature of humanity, uniting the divine nature with the human nature, and thus regained what had been lost. Jesus summed up the development intended by God. This was not merely theological evolution, for Christ remained the Divine Logos. He brought to completion the glory of human nature precisely because he was more than man, the Word of God who assumed the original substance of man. Through Christ, by way of adoption, eternal life is given to human beings, and they are empowered to become all that the Creator intended.

Being empowered to be holy is at the heart of our perception of North American spirituality. It is closely connected with creation and with the coming of the Savior. If we don't need a Savior, God is merely an insurance policy. Our response is not only gratitude; but, more basically, it is love and awe at what God has done for us.

The coming of Christ and our proper response can be illustrated by a story. A man went to visit a friend. Upon arriving at the destination, he discovered that the friend was in the process of moving some large pieces of furniture. He helped the friend all afternoon with the move. At the end of the day, the friend was filled with gratitude. He presumed that being of help was the purpose of the visit, but actually it was only an expression of the true motivation for the visit, which was the love of friendship. Gratitude was a wonderful response, but it fell short of expressing profound relationship.

The love that God has for us is the compelling force that calls us to our true dignity. This has been the experience of our ancestors in religion. Saint Gregory wrote: ''We are bold to say it, God is out of himself by reason of his immense love''; and Saint Thomas wrote: ''God loves mankind just as if people were his god, and as if without people he could not be happy''; Saint Alphonsus also said: ''And now, what delight have I left in heaven, now that I have lost people, who were my delight?'' All of these authors are commenting on the simple verse of Proverbs 8:31: "I found delight in the sons of men."

"God so loved the world that he gave his only Son" (John 3:16). We were saved from sin and we are filled with gratitude, but even more, we are loved and we are filled with love. "Over all these put on love, that is, the bond of perfection" (Colossians 3:14).

Personal considerations

1. How does your job serve to build the kingdom of God on earth?

2. Place some object in your workplace that will symbolically remind you that your work is holy.

CHAPTER 9

Cultivating Holiness

One day, an older priest gave the new associate priest some practical advice. He said, "Don't simply *do* holy things without *being* holy." The young priest wondered what the words meant. How could he administer the sacraments, give religious instructions, or direct parish programs without becoming holy? Only years later did he realize how easily sacred actions can become routine.

The words of the older priest apply not only to the clergy but also to others. All people run the risk of doing things — selling stocks and bonds, doing laundry, rearing children, laughing with friends, listening to homilies, tilling the fields — without the awareness of holiness and therefore, to some extent anyway, not experiencing the fullness of the Christian life. The connection between action and holiness is worthy of consideration.

Do we do holy things in order to *become* holy? To word the question in this way is dangerous. It not only indicates that we are not yet there but also implies that our true nature is not a holy one. Rather, it implies that we must capture our holiness by stockpiling prayers and works of goodness. While we are only too aware of the effects of original sin in our weak natures, we also profess that we, in Baptism, are washed clean and become sons and daughters of God and members of his Church. In our very nature, therefore, because of God's gracious gift, we become holy.

Holiness is not a trait we possess or attain; it is a blessing bestowed on us by God. It is not an edifice that others will be able to see once built; it is a way of being authentic. In fact, then, we do holy things not in order to *become* holy but — following the philosophical principle that our actions flow from our very being — we do holy things because we *are* holy.

We do not earn our salvation; we accept it. It is given to us by the Redeemer. The spiritual life does not consist in living a good life in order to merit reward. It is not even a search for union with God. We have salvation. We have union with God. What then is the goal of the Christian life?

Seeking the meaning of life is not solely a Christian question. It has been asked by reflective people of all generations and all faiths. Even atheists have to wrestle with this problem; like those who seek the fountain of youth, illusions continue to deceive them. The Christian tradition, however, offers an answer.

Saint John of the Cross, among the most respected of mystics, allowed himself to journey into the dark and scarcely charted forest of authentic life. He spoke of *nadas* (Spanish for "nothings"). They form a checklist of possible answers about the meaning of life that he rejected. Unfortunately, we cannot simply walk in his footprints. Each of us has to hack his or her own course, because each experience of life is a little different. But Saint John of the Cross is a sign of hope because for each of us the way is similar. We'll be able to say what life is not before we can say what life is.

Much of human existence is illusory. We set up a grouping of routines, habits, mind-sets, and convictions that help us deal with daily life. We expend a tremendous amount of energy reinforcing these platforms — for fear that our very world would collapse without them. These ideologies give us a way of operating in society; they are actually necessary for human interaction. Sometimes we mutually agree with our fellow citizens that we will do certain things in order to accomplish some task, for instance by drawing up a legal contract; sometimes we merely take for granted that we will agree to act in a certain way, for instance that we will stop at the red light at an intersection. Living together in society demands some ''arbitrary'' agreement.

There are also many under-the-surface beliefs that we take for granted. Why, for instance, does the executive make a salary in six figures while the assembly line worker's salary is in five figures? Does the executive work more? Can the product be built without the laborer? Or is it simply that it was set up that way long ago and we accept it as normal? Why is it that a handsome gentleman has a better chance of getting a good rating in a job interview than an equally or perhaps even better qualified person who does not present himself so well? Is the interviewer not influenced by the assumption that external beauty is a reflection of quality? Why is it that the lady driving a sparkling new four-door V-8 thinks she has more right to be on the road than the driver of the rusty pickup truck? Does she not figure that she is better than the other? ''Power has its privilege,'' ''If you have it flaunt it,'' ''Clothes make the man'' — these are just a few of our underlying assumptions. But they are illusory.

We can even be lost in the illusion that our worthwhile projects are going to solve the problems at hand. The constitution of a great country can be filled with beautifully worded rights and duties, but no matter how precise the wording and penmanship, it remains merely a piece of parchment unless the ideals are enacted.

Even our human relationships can fool us. We too easily get taken in by dependency or by a need to control and hide the reality under the guise of ''love.'' Some of our greatest illusions are disguised in relationships.

The fact still remains that we seem to need some system of assumptions if we are going to exist, and ridding ourselves of our existing illusions will only necessitate replacing them with others.

The point is not to denigrate these realities of life but to take them for what they are worth, or at least to see that they are *nadas,* not the true meaning of life.

The best insight into the true meaning of our lives is probably afforded in the death experience of an integrated person. As the process unfolds, the dying man or woman lets go of one *nada* after another. Things that used to occupy so much attention and demand so much energy are dropped from the baggage the individual has carried through life, like an ocean liner lying still in the water as the barnacles fall off its hull. The grim reality of ''you can't take it with you'' intrudes on the dying person. All that remains is the person himself or herself: only the individual that has been formed by his or her life-long relationships to the world and to its people. This self is what the person will take into eternity, there to be met by God and to share life with other individuals forever.

The meaning of the Christian life is the simplest of all discoveries. It is to walk with our core selves through life and to be authentic. It is to avoid being deluded by illusions, though we have to live within them. Jesus said it directly: ''They do not belong to the world any more than I belong to the world. I do not ask that you take them out of the world but that you keep them from the evil one'' (John 17:14). It is to see beneath the surface, to see God everywhere, to dance in freedom through life, and to know that all our world is set before us so we may be our true selves. ''Blessed are the clean of heart, for they will see God'' (Matthew 5:8).

Personal considerations

1. Do you believe with conviction that Jesus Christ has won your salvation?

2. Imagine that you have only three months to live. What is important to you?

CHAPTER 10
Preparing for Eternity

In times past, God spoke in partial and various ways to our ancestors through the prophets; in these last days, he spoke to us through a son, whom he made heir of all things and through whom he created the universe,

who is the refulgence of his glory,
the very imprint of his being,
and who sustains all things by his mighty word
(Hebrews 1:1-3).

Jesus is the Savior. He has not only shown us the meaning of life, but has empowered us to live authentic lives. He is the Model. In him we have the fullness of revelation, and we repeat within our own bodies his paschal passage through death to resurrection.

Jesus' ministry was a journey toward Jerusalem. "After he had said this, he proceeded on his journey up to Jerusalem" (Luke 19:28). He knew what that meant: "Behold, we are going up to Jerusalem and everything written by the prophets about the Son of Man will be fulfilled. He will be handed over to the Gentiles and he will be mocked and insulted and spat upon; and after they have scourged him they will kill him, but on the third day he will rise" (Luke 18:31-33).

This basic message can be found throughout the Gospels. Jesus knew the negative reaction his teachings and actions aroused in his enemies, but he continued to be faithful to his calling all the way to Jerusalem and death.

Jesus' journey to death, however, is only a part of the revelation of his life. Otherwise, Christianity would be at least a bit masochistic in holding the experience up as a prototype. The picture is rounded out by the promise of Resurrection.

Someone once described original sin as being afraid to die. In the context of death and resurrection, though it isn't a precise theological definition, there is a profound truth in the statement. Because we have a tendency to avoid our daily deaths, we are barred from our daily resurrections; and because we run from death, we do not rest in life. Only through death can we experience resurrection. "For whoever wishes to save his life will lose it, but whoever loses his life for my sake will save it. What profit is there for one to gain the whole world yet lose or forfeit himself?" (Luke 9:24-25).

God does not challenge us to die because he enjoys our struggles or even because he asks us to prove the sincerity of our commitment. Dying is part of abundant living. We have to die to greed and apathy, to violence and exploitation, to hatred and sloth so that we might live. Walls that protect our comfort zones too easily become reinforced; we excuse ourselves too readily from being vulnerable to the risks of relationships. Dying is exactly what we have to do to rise to our full stature. It hurts and we are afraid of dying; yet there is no other way to resurrection. Rising above sin, because sin is unworthy of us, is the real meaning of losing our lives in order to save them.

The example of Jesus, however, goes far beyond merely avoiding sin. It is more radical and internal. It calls us to die to our very selves, to the part of ourselves, trained over many years of self-discovery, that seems to protect and insulate us; it calls us to stop our selfish maneuverings so that the higher parts can thrive. This is actually the birth of our true identity. Nonetheless, the challenge can sound very threatening: "Unless a grain of wheat falls to the ground and dies, it remains just a grain of wheat; but if it dies, it produces much fruit. Whoever loves his life loses it . . . " (John 12:24-25).

We can be our own worst enemy in the growth of the spiritual life. We learn the wrong lessons over our years of experience and in adult Christian life have to face the death of defensive patterns that are not conducive to growth. If we do not allow ourselves to die, we remain just a grain of wheat.

At least three indicators warn that there may be a death required: anger, guilt, and fear. In themselves, of course, these feelings are not wrong, and they may not be indicators of areas of possible growth, but they always merit a second glance.

Justified *anger* is possible, but there are other kinds of anger. A rage because someone accidentally cuts us off in traffic, though he or she caused no damage to us or anyone else, is an indication that we may have to die to a part of ourselves that has inflated our self-importance beyond healthy proportion. *Guilt* over an evil done is one thing, but there are other kinds of guilt. Consternation over whether or not we have offended another by a passing remark is more an indication of preoccupation with self-doubt than concern for another's feelings. *Fear* is an important safeguard for well-being, but it too can get out of hand. Not getting a medical checkup for fear of what may be found is more an indication of the lack of self-confidence than prudence. We do well to die to the manipulations of the ego that paralyze us so that we can come alive.

These examples may seem obvious, but they are only examples to make the point. There are parts of our very selves that require death so that true life may thrive.

Asceticism (the practice of self-denial, self-mortification, and the like) also enters the picture. Our culture is not friendly toward asceticism. We would rather avoid pain if at all possible and certainly are not inclined to choose penitential practices. Yet it is part of the experience of the generations of Christian saints that discipline is required for full life. Control over the amount of sleep, the quality of food, the balance of work and leisure, and of solitude and community all contribute to a sensitivity toward and capacity for the spiritual realities. They are a means toward an end, freely chosen penances that incline us toward fuller life.

But asceticism is wider than getting our own spiritual muscles in shape; it is called for by justice itself. So many of the luxuries that we have grown accustomed to are had at the expense of poorer nations. As our sensitivities increase, so too will the desire to discipline our wants for the sake of those around us.

Jesus' journey to Jerusalem was a serious passage and so this chapter has had to take on some of the serious nuances involved in our preparation for eternity. Death is never easy; but to become depressed over the gravity of this reality misses the point. The Christian message is one of Good News, a Gospel of hope. Death is required but not as an end in itself; it is a means to full life, to resurrection.

Christ did not merely give a vision of what is possible. He gave the power to make the vision real. Rollo May defined power as "the ability to initiate or prohibit change." This is the kind of power we have in the Savior. It is not external force but inner strength given by the Spirit who is with us always. Saint Alphonsus Liguori, reflecting on the reality of the power given to accomplish the task, assured his readers that the Spirit would never fail them. God's grace, as this help was called in the parlance of his day, is always available. For some things, it is true, we need extraordinary grace, which must be requested; but we always have the ordinary grace to ask for the specific extraordinary grace needed. The grace is never refused.

Personal consideration

1. Recall past experiences through which death led to life.

2. Are you preparing properly for eternity? What parts of your life must necessarily die for you to be properly prepared for eternity?

3. Plant a seed and watch its growth to full flower.

CHAPTER 11

Living the Jesus Way

"Before the feast of Passover, Jesus knew that his hour had come to pass from this world to the Father. He loved his own in the world and he loved them to the end" (John 13:1). John's account of Jesus' words at the Last Supper has a profound effect, bringing his Gospel to a climax as they usher in the last hours of the Lord's life. They are spoken in full consciousness that he was about to complete his passage. The urgency of this final message is poignant.

We witness a dialogue about the same topic — loving God and neighbor — in Luke 10:25-28. At the request of Jesus, the lawyer summarized the law with these words: "You shall love the Lord, your God, with all your heart, with all your being, with all your strength, and with all your mind, and your neighbor as yourself." Jesus then said: "Do this and you will live." And in John's Last Discourse, this teaching is dramatized:

So, during supper, fully aware that the Father had put everything into his power and that he had come from God and was returning to God, he [Jesus] rose from supper and took off his outer garments. He took a towel and tied it around his waist. Then he poured water into a basin and began to wash the disciples' feet and dry them with the towel around his waist. . . . So when he had washed their feet [and] put his garments back on and reclined at table again, he said to them, "Do you realize what I have done for you? You call me 'teacher' and 'master,' and rightly so, for indeed I am. If I, therefore, the master and teacher, have washed your feet, you ought to wash one another's feet. I have given you a model to follow, so that as I have done for you, you should also do" (John 13:2-5,12-15).

The great religions of the world offer their disciples a variety of means for reaching perfection. The Gnostics, for instance, say that knowledge is the goal of religion: through it the secrets of the way of passage to the higher realms are learned. For the follower of Christ, there is little doubt that the Way, the Truth, and the Life is Jesus Christ; and life in Jesus is a life of love of God and neighbor.

In just a few sentences, Saint Paul captured the essence of what that kind of life encompasses. We hear the words at so many weddings that there is a chance that they can become too familiar. But they are powerful words:

Love is patient, love is kind. It is not jealous, [love] is not pompous, it is not inflated, it is not rude, it does not seek its own interests, it is not quick-tempered, it does not brood over injury, it does not rejoice over wrongdoing but rejoices with the truth. It bears all things, believes all things, hopes all things, endures all things (1 Corinthians 13:4-7).

Love is adult. Words often associated with "love" are not at home with Paul's definition — words like dependency, control, sentimentality, flattery, manipulation, sensuality. Paul's words are the measure we can use to judge a real love life. Insofar as we

53

cannot claim the qualities described by Paul in our relationships, we are not loving.

Most of us — no, *all* of us — have growth potential in love. None of us is a perfect lover. Paul was the first to understand that! He called that part the "old self" which still has a lot of power even in the lives of those incorporated into Christ. There is a part of each of us that throws temper tantrums, insists on instant gratification, and demands full attention. That part of ourselves has to be recognized and confronted — all of which requires discipline and the sound judgment of our mature selves.

Spirituality is actually an invitation to be integrated and become whole. It places priorities in order and helps distinguish between the important and urgent things that occupy the moments of our days. By delving into the depths of our own inner world we learn to do more than simply tolerate other earth dwellers. Awareness of self spills over into understanding of others and working to change the injustices of our world. Knowing our own stories expands the ability to listen to other stories. Being in touch with the complexity of the self destroys the stereotypes that reduce others to simplistic terms. The life of the Gospel is not merely an ideal, it is the true and complete life of one who is alive in Christ.

Being alive in Christ involves the indwelling of the Holy Spirit. The life of love is possible only because Jesus not only gave us a vision of life but the power to bring that vision to reality. "I tell you the truth, it is better for you that I go. For if I do not go, the Advocate will not come to you. But if I go, I will send him to you. . . . But when he comes, the Spirit of truth, he will guide you to all truth" (John 16:7,13).

The Holy Spirit is shrouded in mystery. We can only imagine the wrinkled foreheads of the apostles when Jesus spoke these words recorded in John's Gospel. No one wants to hear of the exit of a dear one, even though Jesus promised that it was better for us that he go. Something important is being said here.

The Holy Spirit has had the misfortune of being described in functional ways. The Spirit is known as "power" or as "energy," is called the "relationship" between the Father and the Son and the "inspiration" of the prophets, is referred to as "wind," "fire," "coolness in the heat," "solace in woes" — and the Spirit is all these things. But certainly these gifts are not sufficient in themselves to make the apostles want them as a replacement for the person of Jesus himself. There had to be more to it!

The "more to it" is the possibility of the presence of God in the middle — no, at the *very* heart — of daily life. The Holy Spirit is able to sanctify the person indwelt to a greater extent than would have been possible if the Lord had not left the world and sent us the Spirit. And so Jesus could honestly tell his apostles: "If you loved me, you would rejoice that I am going to the Father" (John 14:28).

The closest unity possible between two human beings is the moral union of friendship. As close as this relationship truly is, indwelling — no matter how much it is desired — is not attainable; the two remain always separate. The indwelling of the Holy Spirit, however, exceeds the most perfect human relationship. It is for this reason that Paul glories in the awareness that the Spirit who indwells our hearts knows us better than we know ourselves:

> The Spirit too comes to the aid of our weakness; for we do not know how to pray as we ought, but the Spirit itself intercedes with inexpressible groanings. And the one who searches hearts knows what is the intention of the Spirit, because it intercedes for the holy ones according to God's will (Romans 8:26-27).

The indwelling of the Holy Spirit is our sanctification. It is the union of persons; the indwelling is our holiness, the adoption which makes us cry out and proclaim: "I live, no longer I, but Christ lives in me" (Galatians 2:20).

Adopted son or daughter of the Father, Christ living in us, the indwelling of the Holy Spirit — all of these phrases are real descriptions of the Christian life. They point to a true spirit of humble dependence on God — not a spiritual elitism.

We can delude ourselves into thinking we are in control. We would like to be able to tell God when to work his magic, like a loving parent tells an obedient child when to act. But all is gift which is given so that we can respond, not control. Our Christian journey is to an uncharted distant land, similar to Abraham's trek to a place unknown; it is not patterned, not mapped. Faith is a gift given that enables us to give ourselves to the journey of our lives.

Jesus promised that our joy would be complete in him; but he did not promise that it would be easy. He said to take up the cross and follow him. Living the Jesus way means finding joy while carrying the cross. It means working as though all depends on us and praying as though all depends on God.

Personal considerations

1. List your closest relationships. Taking Paul's definition of love, see how close you come to true love.

2. Extend this description of love to include fellow workers, neighbors, people of other races and creeds. Do you love?

3. To a bowl of water add a drop of food coloring. Consider that your union with God is more thorough than this mixture.

CHAPTER 12
Praying Becomes Christians

A central issue of any booklet that is concerned with the spiritual life has to be prayer. What has been said about the many utterances of God and our varied responses leads up to this essential ingredient in a vital spirituality. Praying celebrates the experience of God and further opens the person to hear the voice of God in daily life.

Prayer has been described in many ways, but all the definitions involve three characteristics: God, the individual praying, and the contact between God and the individual. Prayer can be done in the midst of activity or in the seclusion of any private place. It can be done formally or in spontaneous outbursts of excitement. But always, it is the exchange, the interaction between God and the person praying.

Theologically, prayer is a positive response to a grace from God who invites the individual to enter the dialogue. Humanistically, prayer is the decision to lift up the heart to the Almighty at specific times because it's hard to remember God is present when one has to cross six lanes of the superhighway during rush hour to get off at the proper exit. Prayer is the most direct expression of being in contact with God.

Traditionally, four kinds of prayer are spoken of: praise, thanksgiving, contrition, and petition. Prayer of adoration or praise and prayer of thanksgiving follow experiences of the love of God. These ways of praying are natural expressions of the experiences of awe that flood those who are aware of God's constant presence in their lives and in the world.

Prayer of contrition is another ordinary companion of those who know the gifts of God in this world and the call to use these gifts to become fully alive. Knowing God carries with it an awareness of how poorly we respond to his love, how short of the mark we fall. Prayer of contrition becomes part of our daily prayer. Christians need to ask to be forgiven for not living up to their potential.

Prayer of petition requires a little extra thought. It is, first of all, not selfish. If properly understood, it is not a kind of command or manipulation, like waving a magic wand that orders God to run the world as we see fit or to change the course of the natural flow of the universe. If properly used, prayer of petition does not relieve us of responsibility for using our talents; it channels them to the specific matter of concern.

Here is an example. Suppose a person prays that God will give growth to his or her garden. Does that mean that the gardener expects God to place the correct amount of holy water on the plot in order to bring about a bountiful harvest? God has already offered all that is necessary for growth in the seed and the properly used elements of nature. It is the gardener's task to plant and cultivate and water and harvest. What, then, does such a prayer mean?

Our prayer of petition means first of all that we do not believe that everything is solely the work of our hands. Our task in creation is to cooperate with the Creator who has blessed the universe with tremendous powers and has given dominion over the earth to human beings. God works miracles through the powers he has already placed at our disposal. The hand of God is found by penetrating the mystery of God already present in the world. When we pray, we draw all the forces of God into operation for a specific task, be it garden growth or physical healing. The prayer does not excuse our effort; it focuses the energy of God on a specific end.

Our prayer of petition may not always bring about the result we expect. For instance, if we pray that a particularly nasty neighbor gets a transfer at work and moves from the block, our prayer may effect a change in us rather than a change of address. This prayer is not proper; it is a manipulation. The prayer to bring about a solution to our difficulty may challenge us to face the problem and use all our talents to bring about a Christian solution.

Prayer of petition then gives God great honor. It recognizes that he is the Creator and "holds the whole world in his hands." It also respects our human dignity, bestowed on us by the Creator, and our sacred duty to be stewards of his creation.

In a crisis, our awareness of personal responsibility and the absence of manipulation may not be clear. We tend to panic and look upon petition with near superstition. That's of no real consequence at the time, but an understanding of some of the deeper realities surrounding prayer of petition during times of tranquillity is important.

Although prayer fits in quite nicely with ordinary life and the events that make up our day, a specific time of prayer seems to become more and more important as we become the integrated person offered by the Christian way of life. Most sincere Christians find it necessary to pray daily in some place where there are no interruptions, in a position that is found to be comfortable, usually for about half an hour. The rules are few! When distraction comes, no violence is required. It is simply necessary to recognize that the prayer has ceased and to make a decision to return to the prayer.

Actually, prayer takes on multiple forms, depending on the particular circumstances of the person's life. It may mean being present with God through the rote prayers learned long ago, because we can do nothing but that. Even in the simplest formula, we can centralize our awareness in God. It may be contact through thoughtful meditation because we have to figure something out about life. It may be just a walk, as one foot after the other strikes the concrete of the city street or the country lane. It may be simply sitting in the presence of God.

Prayer is not just a private matter. Public prayer, too, makes up the Christian life. Especially important are the sacraments. Defined traditionally as "outward signs, instituted by Christ, to give grace," they are our guarantees that we are definitely in contact with God. God lives in eternity; we live in time, the chronological progression of moment following moment. For God, all is *now*. In the sacraments, we enter God's time. We enter the ever-present moment. It is Christ who is incorporating us into the Church *now*, who is forgiving our sins *now*, who is healing our illnesses *now*, who is appointing us to our life's tasks *now*, who is nourishing us with his body and blood *now*.

The rituals of the Church have incorporated these wonderful encounters with God and integrated our lives with eternity. For us, this is most often celebrated in the Eucharist. We join as a community, the Body of Christ, to celebrate our Christian meaning. We recall our unworthiness and are forgiven; we are nourished and instructed by the Word of God; we bring to the altar the works of our hands — symbolized in the bread and wine first given to us as raw elements by God but formed by human effort. We offer all and it is accepted, consecrated, and returned to us for our lives. We leave as a community, elevated to a new level, to be the leaven for our world.

We can be the salt of the earth, Christians fully alive to authentic life. Our prayer celebrates this wonder and makes us aware that it is happening to us in this very day. It sanctifies the past and it sets the course for the future. It is rest for our very selves in God.

Prayer need not have any objective; yet the fruits of the prayer become soon apparent. Peace resides in the heart; love of neighbor becomes the way of life; and surety that all's right in heaven and earth, no matter what happens, is the constant conviction of the soul.

In the end, prayer is the introduction and the conclusion of all the matters of this booklet. It is the source and celebration of the integration of all the points made here. *Mourning Becomes Electra* is the name of a classic drama written by Eugene O'Neill; in the same vein we can say that "praying becomes Christians." No Christian can reach home without it.

Personal considerations

1. Do you pray daily, knowing prayer to be the source and celebration of your life?

2. Experiment with quiet prayer. Begin with an act of faith — lasting about thirty seconds — and recall that the God who loves has given the grace to pray; end with a slow two-minute Our Father. Aim for about half an hour of prayer; set an alarm clock so you don't have to worry about the time.

This prayer does not have intellectual content. One word that capsulizes the faith experience is sufficient; repeat it over and over to help you stay in the presence of God. The word could be *God* or *Lord* or *Jesus* or a thousand other possibilities. The prayer is in the heart, not on the tongue. Just rest in the presence of God.

Afterword

The following is a story from ancient rabbinic literature that has been adapted for Catholic readers. It captures the whole point of this booklet on spirituality.

Once upon a time there was a famous bishop. He enjoyed a sterling reputation as a wonderful pastor, superlative preacher, and expert director of souls. As he roamed the countryside with his group of disciples, he always attracted large congregations and his fame continually grew. Nonetheless, like all human beings, he eventually had to face his own death. This he did gracefully and with determination that the good work begun would not end. One by one he called forth his faithful followers and charged them with various duties.

One of his disciples, a man named John, was given the duty of telling the life of the bishop and the message he had preached to all who would listen. John had hoped for a more prestigious position; but the old bishop assured him that after all the stories were told he would live a comfortable life. So John the storyteller fulfilled his task of repeating stories about the bishop.

One day, John heard of a very wealthy man who paid well to hear stories of the bishop. John set out for the man's house. When he arrived, he was welcomed with open arms; but for some strange reason, John could think of no story to tell. The first day passed. On the second day, the wealthy man told John to relax and then eventually a story would return to mind. On the third day, John decided to apologize for his lapse of memory and to leave the man's home: Then suddenly he remembered this story:

The bishop had set out with his disciples for a pagan land, arriving on a day when the sacrifice of a Christian to the fire goddess was to take place. The Christians were hiding in their huts as the bishop walked into the village. Just when the procession was to begin, the bishop stopped at one of the Christian's huts. The head of the household tried to hurry him inside to protect him, but the bishop refused to be hidden. Instead, he stood in the doorway and watched the procession.

Just as the witch doctor approached, the bishop stepped forward and called out firmly, "Come here!" To everyone's surprise, the man obeyed, and he and the bishop talked for some time.

That's how John ended the story, and he apologized that it was such a strange one. It was the last story he could remember about the bishop. He didn't expect much payment for it and rose to go. Surprised, he saw that the wealthy man was crying. Then the man confessed to John, "That story is mine. I was that witch doctor, and the bishop knew me because I was a fallen-away Christian from his church. He told me to leave the country and that I would know I was forgiven when I heard my story. I have paid well to hear every story of the bishop. Now the bishop's prediction has come true. I have heard *my story* and you have told your last story. I am forgiven and you shall live comfortably in my household for the rest of your life."

God's messages are forever around us, and we have heard them many times; but until we hear our *own story,* his messages will always remain outside of us. As Mary, on that first Easter morning, mistook Jesus for the gardener, we run the risk of not recognizing God in our lives. Only when Jesus spoke Mary's own name were her eyes opened. Only when we hear *our story* will our true spirituality begin.

ALSO BY RICHARD BOEVER, C.SS.R.

CAMEOS OF CHURCH HISTORY
This brief survey touches on the most important moments and trends from the first Pentecost to Vatican II, offering a concise, interesting introduction to the roots of our Catholic heritage. **$1.95**

OTHER HELPFUL BOOKS FROM LIGUORI

YOUR SPIRITUAL JOURNEY: Ancient Truths and Modern Insights
by Reverend Thomas E. Legere
Careful research and lively writing make this collection of two-page essays an insightful guide to discovering ourselves as physical, mental, and spiritual beings. Topics considered are both timeless and timely as the author shows how both the wisdom of the ages and modern science can shed light on our spiritual journey. **$3.50**

HOW TO PRAY ALWAYS (Without Always Praying)
by Silvio Fittipaldi
Explaining how prayer is rooted in basic life experience, this book focuses on ways to become more human and more prayerful. Based on Scripture and religious tradition, this book presents prayer as questioning, as wonder, as silence, as grace, and as wisdom. **$2.95**

GROWING IN INNER FREEDOM: A Guide for Today
by Philip St. Romain
Based on the philosophy that "healthy attitudes lead to healthy life experiences," this book offers 40 days — and 40 ways — to greater spiritual freedom. This 40-day program includes suggested practices that will help readers discover their own sense of inner freedom and live their lives to the fullest. **$1.95**

Order from your local bookstore or write to:
Liguori Publications, Box 060, Liguori, Missouri 63057
*(Please add 75¢ for postage and handling for first
item ordered and 25¢ for each additional item.)*